PATSY CLAIRMONT

Collecting STARDUST

A NIGHTTIME JOURNAL

WATERBROOK
PRESS

COLLECTING STARDUST
PUBLISHED BY WATERBROOK PRESS
2375 Telstar Drive, Suite 160
Colorado Springs, Colorado 80920
A division of Random House, Inc.

ISBN 1-57856-429-8

Printed in the United States of America
2000—First Edition

10 9 8 7 6 5 4 3 2 1

Sleepy Friend,

If you are anything like me, there are nights when even if you're weary (yawn), you cannot fall asleep. Thoughts drop in like unexpected visitors, chat endlessly, and keep us from drifting off. I am especially susceptible to mental jabber during exciting, pressure-filled, or sad times. There are seasons when—try as I might—I can't seem to clear today's activities, tomorrow's plans, or troublesome conversations from replaying in my frazzled mind.

Years ago my mom administered to me an elixir that didn't stop the tendencies of my bustling brain, but did direct my thoughts to a quieter place, allowing me health-giving, mind-soothing rest. Her remedy is almost as fun as collecting stardust!

When I was a young girl and couldn't fall asleep, Mom would bring me a tablet (no, not of stone) and a pencil and have me empty the contents of my head onto paper. There was something about having a place for my thoughts—other than rumbling and grumbling around in my noggin—that was not only a relief, but also a release. Then, often after writing my mind clear, I would slip into dreamland.

Today, as one who is deep into adulthood (yes, old), I have more awake evenings in which to practice this homespun recipe. So I keep pen and paper (no, not parchment) on my bedstand, and when my head is bursting with mental adrenaline—when I should be donning p.j.'s and crawling under the covers—I reach for my journal. After placing the loose contents (conscious thoughts) of my mind onto the page, I snuggle into the stardust on my pillow and slip into la-la land.

Does this always work? Of course not, but more times than not it's just what the sandman ordered. Besides, when you reread your ramblings the following day, it can direct you in your prayers. Scripture tells us that our thoughts are not God's thoughts and that we can help bring our minds in line with His as we pray through our writings. (It can alert us to what is troubling, tempting, and taunting us.)

I have found my end-of-the-day tumbling thoughts usually divide quite naturally into two parts: Remembrances (thoughts about events that have already occurred) and Reminders (things I want to make sure I do tomorrow). For me, journaling my thoughts is like giving them an address, allowing me to get back to them another time (preferably during daylight hours).

This journal isn't meant to be a place for the deep, introspective work of your inner life—although feel free to use it that way if you like—but rather a way to relieve your mind from the day's litter. I don't know how your days run, but mine are definitely aerobically active; sometimes I don't stop until I drop into my bed. That is when a myriad of thoughts tend to sweep in. I begin to think of what I didn't get done and things I need to do, and somehow jotting those down in my journal under Reminders takes pressure off my mind. Then, under Remembrances, I write my concerns or assessments of the day (week, month) that are still pressing in on my thoughts. Having accomplished this, I bring closure to my day with a prayer of gratitude and (hopefully) dip into dreamland.

Throughout the journal I have written petite prayers; I hope you'll write some of your own. Written prayer can help us to focus and steady our thoughts. There are also quotes from my book of short stories, *Stardust on My Pillow*, from Scripture, and from other sources that might inspire your own writings.

And now, my friends…may your pillows be covered in stardust and may your dreams be heavenly,

Patsy

P.S. The Collecting Stardust portion of the journal, at the back, is to list your brilliant (at least they all seem brilliant at 2 A.M.) middle-of-the-night ideas or insights that come to you, so they aren't lost. More about that later.

Dear Journal,

I had the strangest dream last night. I found myself in a long room. The walls were lined with glass, but the building had no roof, which allowed the light to be reflected off the myriad pieces of colored glass. Transparent rainbows seemed to fill the room with a warm glow. An angelic being entered, but instead of using the perfect sheets of glass, he took a broom and swept up shards from under the work station, in the corners, and behind the counter. He scooped the fragments into a basket and poured them out onto the table. Then he pulled out some sterling tools from a golden box and leaned over the smudged glass. Some of the shards had rough edges, and some were actually jagged. Many were oddly shaped, and all of them were coated in dust. These were throwaway pieces, ones that had been unsalvageable, ones that had been dropped, walked on, and forgotten.

I don't know how long the angel hovered over his work, but he pursued his objective intently. He softened the jagged corners, reshaped the distorted ones, and polished each broken piece. Then he brought out a form from underneath the table and fit the pieces into it.

I moved closer to see this glass puzzle and was amazed that it took every piece to finish the pattern. I watched as he soldered, each silver seam drawing the pieces together into a design. When he removed the form, he hung the creation on a hook in the center of the room, and then he knelt as though he was praying.

I looked up, and my breath caught in my throat. From all the brokenness he had designed a cross...a dazzling, patchwork cross.

I awoke unsure of all the dream's meaning but certain my wholeness was part of God's ultimate plan.

—FROM "THE KALEIDOSCOPE," *STARDUST ON MY PILLOW*

"I have seen his ways, but I will heal him; I will guide him and restore comfort to him, creating praise on the lips of the mourners in Israel. Peace, peace, to those far and near," says the LORD. "And I will heal them."

—ISAIAH 57:18-19

Remembrances

_____

_____

_____

_____

_____

_____

_____

_____

_____

_____

_____

_____

_____

Reminders

_____

_____

_____

_____

Another day is done, and You, Lord, have once again seen
fit to guide our paths. As we lay our heads upon our pillows,
we do so with the assurance that You long to quiet our minds.
Thank You for the comforting promise that You will always,
always, always be there for those we love and for us. Amen.

The LORD watches over you—the LORD is your shade at your right hand; the sun will not harm you by day, nor the moon by night. The LORD will keep you from all harm—he will watch over your life; the LORD will watch over your coming and going both now and forevermore.

—PSALM 121:5-8

Remembrances

_____

_____

_____

_____

_____

_____

_____

_____

_____

_____

_____

_____

_____

_____

_____

_____

_____

_____

_____

_____

_____
_____
_____
_____
_____
_____
_____
_____
_____
_____

Reminders

_____
_____
_____
_____
_____

Dearest Watcher, _____

_____
_____
_____
_____
_____
_____
_____
_____

The heavens declare the glory of God; the skies proclaim the work of his hands. Day after day they pour forth speech; night after night they display knowledge. There is no speech or language where their voice is not heard. Their voice goes out into all the earth, their words to the ends of the world.

—PSALM 19:1-4

Remembrances

_____

_____

_____

_____

_____

_____

_____

_____

_____

_____

Reminders

_____

_____

_____

_____

_____

Dear Heavenly Creator, _____

_____

_____

_____

_____

_____

_____

_____

She's a caring woman. Yes, a real servant to others. Why, folks
around these parts thinks mighty highly of her. I think that's
because she's more full of Jesus than she is of herself.

—FROM "CHATTANOOGA CHOO-CHOO," *STARDUST ON MY PILLOW*

Remembrances

_____

_____

_____

_____

_____

_____

_____

_____

_____

_____

_____

_____

_____

_____

_____

_____

_____

_____

_____

_____

_____

_____

_____

_____

_____

_____
_____
_____
_____
_____
_____
_____
_____
_____
_____
_____

Reminders

_____
_____
_____
_____
_____

Dear Jesus, _____
_____
_____
_____
_____
_____
_____
_____
_____

The heavens call to you, and circle around you, displaying to you their eternal splendours, and your eye gazes only to earth.

—DANTE, *THE DIVINE COMEDY*

Remembrances

_____
_____
_____
_____
_____
_____
_____
_____
_____
_____

Reminders

_____
_____
_____
_____
_____

Father, I am focused on earth instead of You...

_____
_____
_____
_____
_____
_____
_____

He who dwells in the shelter of the Most High will rest in the shadow of the Almighty. I will say of the LORD, "He is my refuge and my fortress, my God, in whom I trust."… He will cover you with his feathers, and under his wings you will find refuge; his faithfulness will be your shield and rampart. You will not fear the terror of night, nor the arrow that flies by day.

—PSALM 91:1-2,4-5

Remembrances

Reminders

O Lord God, my refuge and my fortress, _____

Where were you when I laid the earth's foundation? Tell me, if you understand. Who marked off its dimensions? Surely you know! Who stretched a measuring line across it? On what were its footings set, or who laid its cornerstone—while the morning stars sang together and all the angels shouted for joy?

—JOB 38:4-7

Remembrances

_____

_____

_____

_____

_____

_____

_____

_____

_____

_____

_____

_____

_____

_____

_____

_____

_____

_____

_____

_____

_____

_____

_____

_____

_____

_____

_____

_____

_____

_____

_____

Reminders

_____

_____

_____

_____

_____

_____

Father God, sometimes I want to be in control and forget that You are...

_____

_____

_____

_____

_____

_____

_____

_____

"Is it well with you?" the old man asked as he stepped closer to the bedside.

"As well as can be," Emanuel said in a voice filled with both sadness and promise.

"How might I ease your pain?" the old man inquired.

"Sit and tell me of yourself," the invalid said.

The old man filled the pail and set it back near Emanuel's bedside, placing the dipper at his patient's fingertips. Then, with some effort, the old man pulled a wooden chair next to the bedside and sat down.

"What shall I tell you today?"

"Tell me of her, the Woman of the Chapel."

"But we talked of her yesterday."

"Yes, yes. I know. Tell me again."

The old man put his face in his hands for several moments to steady his thoughts and then, lifting his head, he began. "She was lovely. Her raven hair caught the sun as she worked in the fields. Her eyes were full of tender mercies, and her hands were gentle and strong. She was a wisp of a woman with mightiness at her core; her spirit drew the people to her. Each evening, after the fields, she would go to the chapel where workers would ask her to pray for them and their families. They would bring their children, and she would enfold them in her arms and whisper up prayers like sweet incense. Sick children would be strengthened, frantic babies would become still in her arms, and families would be drawn together in her presence."

—FROM "THE WOMAN OF THE CHAPEL," *STARDUST ON MY PILLOW*

Remembrances

_____
_____
_____
_____
_____
_____
_____
_____

Reminders

_____
_____
_____
_____
_____

O Father of tender mercies, _____

_____
_____
_____
_____
_____
_____
_____

*Reverie is not a mind vacuum. It is rather the gift of an hour
which knows the plenitude of the soul.*

—GASTON BACHELARD, *THE POETICS OF REVERIE*

Remembrances

I am so exhausted I'm wide awake. I'm even tired of my own voice. Lord, do you feel like talking? How about if I just lie here quietly and listen…for a change? Amen.

Praise the LORD. Praise the LORD from the heavens, praise him in the heights above. Praise him, all his angels, praise him, all his heavenly hosts. Praise him, sun and moon, praise him, all you shining stars. Praise him, you highest heavens and you waters above the skies. Let them praise the name of the LORD, for he commanded and they were created. He set them in place for ever and ever; he gave a decree that will never pass away.

—PSALM 148:1-6

Remembrances

_____
_____
_____
_____
_____
_____
_____
_____
_____
_____
_____
_____
_____
_____
_____
_____
_____
_____
_____

_____

_____

_____

_____

_____

_____

_____

_____

_____

_____

Reminders

_____

_____

_____

_____

_____

I praise You, my Father, for all You have done for me and given me… _____

_____

_____

_____

_____

_____

_____

But at that time your people—everyone whose name is found written in the book—will be delivered.… Those who are wise will shine like the brightness of the heavens, and those who lead many to righteousness, like the stars for ever and ever.

—DANIEL 12:1,3

Remembrances

_____

_____

_____

_____

_____

_____

_____

_____

_____

_____

_____

_____

_____

_____

_____

_____

_____

_____

_____

_____

_____

_____

_____

_____

_____

_____

_____

_____

_____

_____

Reminders

_____

_____

_____

_____

_____

_____

O Deliverer, _____

_____

_____

_____

_____

_____

_____

_____

Remember when we were kids and life was too painful? We'd make a beeline for Dad, and he'd tend to our problems. Somehow he knew exactly what to do. Well, my friend Cyndi says God wants to be that kind of father and more to us. I've had a lot of time to think and even to pray out here in the woods. Yes, your brother prays. I don't have things figured out, but I have a growing sense that our lives were meant to have divine purpose. What do you think?

Love, JW

—FROM "POSTCARDS," *STARDUST ON MY PILLOW*

Remembrances

_____

_____

_____

_____

_____

_____

_____

_____

_____

_____

_____

_____

_____

_____

_____

_____

_____

_____
_____
_____
_____
_____
_____
_____
_____
_____
_____

Reminders

_____
_____
_____
_____
_____

Dear Abba, help me find my divine purpose...

_____
_____
_____
_____
_____
_____
_____
_____

God owns heaven but He craves the earth.

—ANNE SEXTON, *THE AWFUL ROVING TOWARD GOD*

Remembrances

_____

_____

_____

_____

_____

_____

_____

_____

_____

_____

_____

_____

_____

_____

_____

_____

_____

_____

_____

_____

_____

_____

_____

_____

_____

_____

_____

_____
_____
_____
_____
_____
_____
_____
_____
_____
_____

Reminders

_____
_____
_____
_____
_____

Heavenly God, thank You for craving a relationship with me…

_____
_____
_____
_____
_____
_____
_____

Moses said to the LORD, "You have been telling me, 'Lead these people,' but you have not let me know whom you will send with me. You have said, 'I know you by name and you have found favor with me.' If you are pleased with me, teach me your ways so I may know you and continue to find favor with you. Remember that this nation is your people." The LORD replied, "My Presence will go with you, and I will give you rest."

—EXODUS 33:12-14

Remembrances

_____

_____

_____

_____

_____

_____

_____

_____

_____

_____

_____

_____

_____

_____

_____

_____

_____

_____

_____

_____

_____
_____
_____
_____
_____
_____
_____
_____
_____
_____
_____
_____
_____

Reminders

_____
_____
_____
_____
_____

Some days are convoluted and leave our minds in knots—Lord, please untie our thoughts and still our jangled nerves with the soothing balm of Your presence. Only You can reach the deep places of our hearts and set them at peace. We trust You to do that. Amen.

Do everything without complaining or arguing, so that you may become blameless and pure, children of God without fault in a crooked and depraved generation, in which you shine like the stars in the universe as you hold out the word of life.

—PHILIPPIANS 2:14-16

Remembrances

_____
_____
_____
_____
_____
_____
_____
_____
_____
_____

Reminders

_____
_____
_____
_____
_____

Forgive me, Jesus, for my grumbling today...

_____
_____
_____
_____
_____
_____
_____

Dr. Atkins studied her for a moment and then said, "You're
more vulnerable when you're dealing with old wounds, and it
would be easy to want a gentle man, someone unlike your
daddy, to soothe your hurting heart. What you need long-term is
not soothing but healing and closure. That's not to say that gentle
people in your life wouldn't help; we all respond to kindness. Just
don't expect others to erase your interior pain for you."
—FROM "THE KALEIDOSCOPE," *STARDUST ON MY PILLOW*

Remembrances

_____

_____

_____

_____

_____

_____

_____

_____

_____

_____

_____

_____

_____

_____

_____

_____

_____

_____

_____
_____
_____
_____
_____
_____
_____
_____
_____
_____

Reminders

_____
_____
_____
_____
_____

O Gentle Healer, _____

_____
_____
_____
_____
_____
_____
_____
_____

What I like in a good author isn't what he says, but what he whispers.

—LOGAN PEARSALL SMITH, *AFTERTHOUGHTS*

Remembrances

_____

_____

_____

_____

_____

_____

_____

_____

_____

Reminders

_____

_____

_____

_____

_____

Whisper to me, Lord, tonight. Tell me of . . . ____

_____

_____

_____

_____

_____

_____

_____

_____

Can you bind the beautiful Pleiades? Can you loose the cords of Orion? Can you bring forth the constellations in their seasons or lead out the Bear with its cubs? Do you know the laws of the heavens? Can you set up God's dominion over the earth?

—JOB 38:31-33

Remembrances

_____
_____
_____
_____
_____
_____
_____
_____
_____
_____

Reminders

_____
_____
_____
_____
_____

O Mighty and Wonderful God, _____

_____
_____
_____
_____
_____
_____
_____

Give thanks to the Lord of lords: His love endures forever.

to him who alone does great wonders, His love endures forever.

who by his understanding made the heavens, His love endures
  forever.

who spread out the earth upon the waters, His love endures
  forever.

*who made the great lights—*His love endures forever.

the sun to govern the day, His love endures forever.

the moon and stars to govern the night; His love endures forever.

—PSALM 136:3-9

Remembrances

_____

_____

_____

_____

_____

_____

_____

_____

_____

_____

_____

_____

_____

_____

_____

_____

_____

_____

_____

_____

_____

_____

_____

_____

_____

_____

_____

_____

_____

_____

Reminders

_____

_____

_____

_____

_____

Thank You for starlight, Lord, for it reminds us
that while we rest, You're still awake looking out for our best
interests. What a relief. Now as we drift off, we direct our sleepy
thoughts toward You, who hold our world in place… Good
night, dear Savior… See You in the morning. Amen.

One never knows, dear, how one's heart might change direction.
—FROM "ALL THAT JAZZ," *STARDUST ON MY PILLOW*

Remembrances

_____
_____
_____
_____
_____
_____
_____
_____
_____
_____
_____
_____
_____
_____
_____
_____
_____
_____
_____
_____
_____
_____
_____
_____
_____
_____

_____
_____
_____
_____
_____
_____
_____
_____
_____
_____

Reminders

_____
_____
_____
_____
_____

Show me the way, Lord, _____

_____
_____
_____
_____
_____
_____
_____

Prosperity is the blessing of the Old Testament; adversity is the blessing of the New.

—FRANCIS BACON, *ESSAYS*

Remembrances

_____
_____
_____
_____
_____
_____
_____
_____
_____
_____

Reminders

_____
_____
_____
_____

God, help me to see Your light as I face adversity... _____

_____
_____
_____
_____
_____
_____
_____

When I consider your heavens, the work of your fingers, the moon and the stars, which you have set in place, what is man that you are mindful of him, the son of man that you care for him? You made him a little lower than the heavenly beings and crowned him with glory and honor.... O LORD, our Lord, how majestic is your name in all the earth!

—PSALM 8:3-5,9

Remembrances

_____
_____
_____
_____
_____
_____
_____
_____
_____
_____

Reminders

_____
_____
_____
_____
_____
_____

Majestic One, _____
_____
_____
_____
_____
_____
_____
_____

On my bed I remember you; I think of you through the watches of the night. Because you are my help, I sing in the shadow of your wings. My soul clings to you; your right hand upholds me.

—PSALM 63:6-8

Remembrances

_____

_____

_____

_____

_____

_____

_____

_____

_____

_____

_____

_____

_____

_____

_____

_____

_____

_____

_____

_____

_____

_____
_____
_____
_____
_____
_____
_____
_____
_____
_____

Reminders

_____
_____
_____
_____
_____

Thank You for watching over me, Father, _____

_____
_____
_____
_____
_____
_____
_____
_____

*Even now, ever so many years later, some nights moonlight streams
in the windows of my little house and fills it with stardust. I move
my pillow until it's covered and then fall asleep smiling.*

—FROM "STARDUST," *STARDUST ON MY PILLOW*

Remembrances

_____

_____

_____

_____

_____

_____

_____

_____

_____

_____

_____

_____

_____

_____

_____

_____

_____

_____

_____

_____

_____

_____

_____

_____

_____

_____

_____

_____

_____

_____

_____

_____

Reminders

_____

_____

_____

_____

_____

The sun has set and according to Your design, Lord,
nightfall has settled in upon the land. Thank You for giving us a
time to sleep lest we try to run without reserves. Without reserves,
our lamps flicker and go out before our days are done. So in
peace we lie down to rest, trusting You to accomplish what You've
begun. Amen.

It is awfully easy to be hard-boiled about everything in the day-time, but at night it is another thing.

—ERNEST HEMINGWAY, *THE SUN ALSO RISES*

Remembrances

_____

_____

_____

_____

_____

_____

_____

_____

_____

_____

Reminders

_____

_____

_____

_____

_____

Lord, I am troubled... _____

_____

_____

_____

_____

_____

_____

_____

In the heavens he has pitched a tent for the sun, which is like a bridegroom coming forth from his pavilion, like a champion rejoicing to run his course.

—PSALM 19:4-5

Remembrances

_____

_____

_____

_____

_____

_____

_____

_____

_____

_____

_____

_____

_____

_____

_____

_____

_____

_____

_____

_____

_____

_____

_____
_____
_____
_____
_____
_____
_____
_____
_____
_____

Reminders

_____
_____
_____
_____
_____

Heavenly Bridegroom, _____

_____
_____
_____
_____
_____
_____
_____
_____

The LORD gives strength to his people; the LORD blesses his people with peace.

—PSALM 29:11

Remembrances

_____

_____

_____

_____

_____

_____

_____

_____

_____

_____

_____

_____

_____

_____

_____

_____

_____

_____

_____

_____

_____

_____

_____

_____

_____

_____
_____
_____
_____
_____
_____
_____
_____
_____
_____

Reminders

_____
_____
_____
_____
_____
_____

Prince of Peace, _____
_____
_____
_____
_____
_____
_____
_____

Grandma was putting empty milk jugs on wooden stakes to scare any rabbits that might meander into the garden and suggested Sarah help. While they worked, Sarah mentioned she didn't like Twila.

"Why, Sarah?" Grandma asked, her eyes searching Sarah's.

"Oh, she brags too much. You know, like about her straight A's and stuff." Sarah avoided Grandma's gaze.

"Wee one, bad thoughts about folks are like weeds. Left unattended they will take over the garden and choke the life out of it." Then wouldn't you know it, Grandma switched Sarah's duty to weed control for the rest of the week. Probably so Sarah would get the point. Sarah figured she should probably never have told Grandma.

—FROM "GRANDMA MOSES," *STARDUST ON MY PILLOW*

Remembrances

Reminders

_____

_____

_____

_____

_____

Father, don't let me be choked by the weeds in my heart... _____

_____

_____

_____

_____

_____

_____

Belief consists in accepting the affirmations of the soul; unbelief, in denying them.

—RALPH WALDO EMERSON, *REPRESENTATIVE MEN*

Remembrances

_____

_____

_____

_____

_____

_____

_____

_____

_____

_____

_____

_____

_____

_____

_____

_____

_____

_____

_____

_____

_____

_____

_____

_____

_____

_____

_____

_____

_____

_____

_____

_____

_____

_____

_____

Reminders

_____

_____

_____

_____

_____

Tonight as I lie in bed, moonbeams touch my arm,
and I wonder as I watch the dappled light dance across my
hand if it is one more way You stir us to remember You.
Thank You for gentle reminders... Help us not to miss them.
Amen.

Come to me, all you who are weary and burdened, and I will give you rest. Take my yoke upon you and learn from me, for I am gentle and humble in heart, and you will find rest for your souls. For my yoke is easy and my burden is light.

—MATTHEW 11:28-30

Remembrances

_____

_____

_____

_____

_____

_____

_____

_____

_____

_____

_____

_____

_____

_____

_____

_____

_____

_____

_____

_____

_____

_____

_____

_____
_____
_____
_____
_____
_____
_____
_____
_____
_____

Reminders

_____
_____
_____
_____
_____
_____

Jesus, I am weary... _____
_____
_____
_____
_____
_____
_____
_____

Peace I leave with you; my peace I give you. I do not give to you as the world gives. Do not let your hearts be troubled and do not be afraid.

—JOHN 14:27

Remembrances

_____

_____

_____

_____

_____

_____

_____

_____

_____

_____

_____

_____

_____

_____

_____

_____

_____

_____

_____

_____

_____
_____
_____
_____
_____
_____
_____
_____
_____
_____

Reminders

_____
_____
_____
_____
_____

Jesus, I am afraid... _____
_____
_____
_____
_____
_____
_____
_____

The best way to grow out of small is to stand up tall. You don't have to feel brave to act brave.

—FROM "CHATTANOOGA CHOO-CHOO," *STARDUST ON MY PILLOW*

Remembrances

_____

_____

_____

_____

_____

_____

_____

_____

_____

_____

_____

_____

_____

_____

_____

_____

_____

_____

_____

_____

_____

_____

_____

_____

_____

_____

_____

_____

_____

_____

_____

_____

_____

_____

_____

Reminders

_____

_____

_____

_____

_____

_____

Help me to stand tall, God, _____

_____

_____

_____

_____

_____

_____

No pen, no ink, no table, no room, no time, no quiet, no inclination.

—JAMES JOYCE, *LETTERS OF JAMES JOYCE*

Remembrances

_____

_____

_____

_____

_____

_____

_____

_____

_____

_____

_____

God, sometimes I am so disillusioned I can't even write or
pray... _____

_____

_____

_____

_____

_____

_____

_____

And God said, "Let there be lights in the expanse of the sky to separate the day from the night, and let them serve as signs to mark seasons and days and years, and let them be lights in the expanse of the sky to give light on the earth." And it was so.

—Genesis 1:14-15

Remembrances

_____

_____

_____

_____

_____

_____

_____

_____

_____

_____

_____

_____

_____

_____

_____

_____

_____

_____

_____

_____

_____

_____

_____

_____

_____

_____

_____

_____

_____

_____

_____

_____

Reminders

_____

_____

_____

_____

When You pressed the diamond stars

deep into the velvet night, did it make You smile, Lord? Did You throw back Your head at the stunning sight and shake the foundation of the world with holy laughter? And, by the way, who drew the smile on the moon? So many questions... One glorious day You'll tell us the answers and much more. Now I'm the one smiling... What a pleasing way to fall asleep. Amen.

After Jesus was born in Bethlehem in Judea, during the time of
King Herod, Magi from the east came to Jerusalem and asked,
"Where is the one who has been born king of the Jews? We saw
his star in the east and have come to worship him."

—MATTHEW 2:2

Remembrances

_____

_____

_____

_____

_____

_____

_____

_____

_____

_____

_____

_____

_____

_____

_____

_____

_____

_____

_____

_____

_____

_____
_____
_____
_____
_____
_____
_____
_____
_____
_____

Reminders

_____
_____
_____
_____
_____

Precious Savior, born for me over two thousand years ago...

_____
_____
_____
_____
_____
_____
_____

I heard children running and laughing in a distant hall. I held back and listened. One child called out to the other as he ran, "I'm going to hide. Bet you can't find me." I closed my door and slid to the floor. "Oh, God, please find me. Be my Deliverer. Rescue me from the stronghold of fear and teach me what it means to make You my refuge."

—FROM "CLOISTERED," *STARDUST ON MY PILLOW*

Remembrances

_____

_____

_____

_____

_____

_____

_____

_____

_____

_____

_____

_____

_____

_____

_____

_____

_____

_____

_____

_____

_____

_____

_____
_____
_____
_____
_____
_____
_____
_____
_____
_____

Reminders

_____
_____
_____
_____
_____

Deliverer, _____
_____
_____
_____
_____
_____
_____
_____

*The process of writing has something infinite about it. Even
though it is interrupted each night, it is one single notation.*

—ELIAS CANETTI, *THE SECRET HEART OF THE CLOCK*

Remembrances

_____

_____

_____

_____

_____

_____

_____

_____

_____

_____

Reminders

_____

_____

_____

_____

_____

Infinite God, _____

_____

_____

_____

_____

_____

_____

_____

For he received honor and glory from God the Father when the voice came to him from the Majestic Glory, saying, "This is my Son, whom I love; with him I am well pleased." We ourselves heard this voice that came from heaven when we were with him on the sacred mountain. And we have the word of the prophets made more certain, and you will do well to pay attention to it, as to a light shining in a dark place, until the day dawns and the morning star rises in your hearts.

—2 PETER 1:17-19

Remembrances

_____

_____

_____

_____

_____

_____

_____

_____

_____

_____

_____

_____

_____

_____

_____

_____

_____

_____

_____

_____

_____

_____

_____

_____

_____

_____

_____

_____

_____

Reminders

_____

_____

_____

_____

_____

Majestic Glory, _____

_____

_____

_____

_____

_____

_____

_____

I will lie down and sleep in peace, for you alone, O LORD, make me dwell in safety.

—PSALM 4:8

Remembrances

_____

_____

_____

_____

_____

_____

_____

_____

_____

_____

_____

_____

_____

_____

_____

_____

_____

_____

_____

_____

_____

_____

_____

_____

_____

_____

_____

_____

_____

_____

_____

_____

_____

Reminders

_____

_____

_____

_____

Tonight I felt the rumble of thunder
shake my bed, and I watched my room flash with streaks of
lightning that dashed lickety-split across the heavens. I snuggled
deeper under the covers and listened to the windy rain. In the
midst of the storm, a sense of safety filled me… How reassuring,
Lord, to know You are there. Amen.

"Change always takes courage," Cliffton said. "Remember what
you called me when we first met? Brave. It was a brave thing you
did to take a risk and follow your dream, Nichole. But now, child,
you have a greater calling: to find where your heart is at home. If
you hadn't come here, you would still be in Pinckney, keeping your
life on hold, waiting for your dreams to come true. Sometimes we
can't know what we want until we have a way to measure it
through other experiences. Now you can return wiser and braver."

—FROM "ALL THAT JAZZ," *STARDUST ON MY PILLOW*

Remembrances

_____

_____

_____

_____

_____

_____

_____

_____

_____

Reminders

_____

_____

_____

_____

Lord, help me to be brave and follow my dreams and my heart...

_____

_____

_____

_____

_____

_____

_____

The blank page gives the right to dream.

—GASTON BACHELARD, *THE POETICS OF REVERIE*

Remembrances

_____
_____
_____
_____
_____
_____
_____
_____
_____

Reminders

_____
_____
_____
_____
_____
_____

Speak to me, Father, _____
_____
_____
_____
_____
_____
_____
_____

*I rise before dawn and cry for help; I have put my hope in your
word. My eyes stay open through the watches of the night, that I
may meditate on your promises. Hear my voice in accordance
with your love; preserve my life, O LORD, according to your laws.*

—PSALM 119:147-149

Remembrances

_____

_____

_____

_____

_____

_____

_____

_____

_____

_____

_____

_____

_____

_____

_____

_____

_____

_____

_____

_____

_____

_____

_____

_____

_____

_____

_____

_____

_____

_____

_____

_____

Reminders

_____

_____

_____

_____

_____

_____

Renew me, fill me, guide me, Heavenly Father,

_____

_____

_____

_____

_____

_____

_____

I have told you these things, so that in me you may have peace. In this world you will have trouble. But take heart! I have overcome the world.

—JOHN 16:33

Remembrances

_____

_____

_____

_____

_____

_____

_____

_____

_____

_____

_____

_____

_____

_____

_____

_____

_____

_____

_____

_____

_____

_____

_____

_____
_____
_____
_____
_____
_____
_____
_____
_____

Reminders

_____
_____
_____
_____
_____
_____

O King of kings, _____
_____
_____
_____
_____
_____
_____
_____

...man leaned forward, placing his gnarled hand on the ...an's head. "May peace reign in your mind and Christ ...rt."

— FROM "THE WOMAN OF THE CHAPEL," *STARDUST ON MY PILLOW*

Remembrances

_____

_____

_____

_____

_____

_____

_____

_____

_____

_____

_____

_____

_____

_____

_____

_____

_____

_____

_____

_____

_____

_____

_____

_____

_____

_____

_____

_____

_____

_____

_____

_____

_____

_____

_____

_____

_____

_____

Reminders

_____

_____

_____

_____

_____

Lord, thank You for those delicious moments
when I'm conscious that I'm drifting off to sleep—it's as if I have
one foot on earth and one in heaven. It's comforting to know
that our night's rest is in Your starlit presence. Amen.

gives rest but the sincere search for truth.

—PASCAL, *PENSÉES*

Remembrances

_____

_____

_____

_____

_____

_____

_____

_____

_____

_____

_____

_____

_____

_____

_____

_____

_____

_____

_____

_____

_____

_____

_____

_____

_____

_____

_____

_____

_____

_____

_____

_____

_____

_____

_____

_____

Reminders

_____

_____

_____

_____

Assist me in finding the truth of the matter, Lord,

so that I may rest... _____

_____

_____

_____

_____

_____

_____

t peace gives life to the body, but envy rots the bones.

—PROVERBS 14:30

Remembrances

_____

_____

_____

_____

_____

_____

_____

_____

_____

_____

_____

_____

_____

_____

_____

_____

_____

_____

_____

_____

_____

_____

_____

_____

_____

_____

_____
_____
_____
_____
_____
_____
_____
_____
_____
_____

Reminders

_____
_____
_____
_____
_____

Please forgive me of my sins now, Father, including envy
and…   _____
_____
_____
_____
_____
_____
_____
_____

eyes and look to the heavens: Who created all these?
...ings out the starry host one by one, and calls them
...e. Because of his great power and mighty strength,
...nem is missing.

—Isaiah 40:26

Remembrances

_____

_____

_____

_____

_____

_____

_____

_____

_____

_____

_____

_____

_____

_____

_____

_____

_____

_____

_____

_____

_____

_____
_____
_____
_____
_____
_____
_____
_____
_____
_____

Reminders

_____
_____
_____
_____
_____
_____

Creator, _____
_____
_____
_____
_____
_____
_____
_____
_____

Dear Char,

This God stuff is all new to me, but perhaps God can use even your broken heart for some divine design. Remember the summer I broke my arm playing baseball, and the doctor told us that when my arm healed the bone would be stronger than before? I'm thinking that could be true of your heart.

Love, JW

—FROM "POSTCARDS," *STARDUST ON MY PILLOW*

Remembrances

_____
_____
_____
_____
_____
_____
_____
_____
_____
_____

Reminders

_____
_____
_____
_____
_____

O Balm to my soul, _____
_____
_____
_____
_____
_____
_____
_____

It is easier to accept the message of the stars than the message of the salt desert. The stars speak of man's insignificance in the long eternity of time; the desert speaks of his insignificance right now.

—EDWIN WAY TEALE, *AUTUMN ACROSS AMERICA*

Remembrances

_____

_____

_____

_____

_____

_____

_____

_____

_____

_____

_____

Reminders

_____

_____

_____

_____

_____

Tonight a dozen fireflies took turns lighting their
lanterns in my backyard; their intermittent show dazzled me.
*Then a shooting star streaked across the sky, showering stardust in
its trail. And, as if that were not enough, a slice of speckled moon
cast a pool of light over my maple tree, causing it to shimmer. I'm
impressed… Thank You. Amen.*

This is what the LORD says: "Stand at the crossroads and look;
ask for the ancient paths, ask where the good way is, and walk
in it, and you will find rest for your souls."

—JEREMIAH 6:16

Remembrances

_____
_____
_____
_____
_____
_____
_____
_____
_____
_____

Reminders

_____
_____
_____
_____
_____

O Ancient of Days, _____

_____
_____
_____
_____
_____
_____
_____

God keep you in the night, wake you with a song, may you know His delight, to Him you belong.

—FROM "THE WOMAN OF THE CHAPEL," *STARDUST ON MY PILLOW*

Remembrances

_____

_____

_____

_____

_____

_____

_____

_____

_____

_____

_____

_____

_____

_____

_____

_____

_____

_____

_____

_____

_____

_____

_____

_____

_____

_____

_____

_____

_____

_____

_____

_____

Reminders

_____

_____

_____

_____

_____

_____

What joy it is to belong to You, Savior. Help me to
awake each morning with a song on my heart… _____

_____

_____

_____

_____

_____

_____

Oh, Lord, I'm a mess. I can't decide what to feel.... I'm uncertain of what to do now that the gate of my life has been thrown open so wide. I feel like a child who has gone from her wading pool to the ocean's edge: thrilled yet threatened. Please take my hand; don't let me drown.

—FROM "THE WEDDING RING," *STARDUST ON MY PILLOW*

Remembrances

_____

_____

_____

_____

_____

_____

_____

_____

_____

_____

_____

_____

_____

_____

_____

_____

_____

_____

_____

_____

_____

_____
_____
_____
_____
_____
_____
_____
_____
_____
_____
_____

Reminders

_____
_____
_____
_____
_____

The world is big, Lord, with so much to offer. I am excited and yet
scared. Show me… _____
_____
_____
_____
_____
_____
_____

There is no way to peace. Peace is the way.

—A. J. MUSTE, QUOTED IN THE *NEW YORK TIMES*

Remembrances

_____
_____
_____
_____
_____
_____
_____
_____
_____
_____

Reminders

_____
_____
_____
_____

Too often I try to find the way to peace rather than let
You, the Prince of Peace, rule in my heart... _____

_____
_____
_____
_____
_____
_____

The fruit of righteousness will be peace; the effect of righteousness will be quietness and confidence forever. My people will live in peaceful dwelling places, in secure homes, in undisturbed places of rest.

—Isaiah 32:17-18

Remembrances

_____

_____

_____

_____

_____

_____

_____

_____

_____

_____

_____

_____

_____

_____

_____

_____

Reminders

_____

_____

_____

_____

_____

I can hardly hold my thoughts... together...I'm so sleepy. Would You mind, Lord, if we...talked...in the morning? Zzz...oh yes, amen...zzz...

You are all sons of the light and sons of the day. We do not belong to the night or to the darkness. So then, let us not be like others, who are asleep, but let us be alert and self-controlled. For those who sleep, sleep at night, and those who get drunk, get drunk at night. But since we belong to the day, let us be self-controlled, putting on faith and love as a breastplate, and the hope of salvation as a helmet.

—1 THESSALONIANS 5:5-8

Remembrances

_____

_____

_____

_____

_____

_____

_____

_____

_____

_____

_____

Reminders

_____

_____

_____

_____

_____

Lord, help me to be a child of the light. Arm me to do battle
with the dark… _____

_____

_____

_____

_____

_____

_____

_____

Her voice was like a brook singing of its Maker. People listened
carefully to what she said, for the wisdom of the ages rested on
her tongue. She spoke of heaven and hardships in one breath,
knowing one would help us overcome the other. Wherever she
went, birds sang and children laughed.

—FROM "THE WOMAN OF THE CHAPEL," *STARDUST ON MY PILLOW*

Remembrances

_____
_____
_____
_____
_____
_____
_____
_____
_____
_____

Reminders

_____
_____
_____
_____
_____

O God, mold me into Your image so that I may be an
inspiration to others… _____
_____
_____
_____
_____
_____
_____

The angels are so enamoured of the language that is spoken in heaven, that they will not distort their lips with the hissing and unmusical dialects of men, but speak their own, whether there be any who understand it or not.

—RALPH WALDO EMERSON, *ESSAYS*

Remembrances

_____

_____

_____

_____

_____

_____

_____

_____

_____

_____

_____

_____

_____

_____

_____

_____

_____

_____

_____

_____

_____

_____
_____
_____
_____
_____
_____
_____
_____

Reminders

_____
_____
_____
_____
_____

Unimaginable King of an unimaginable heaven,

_____
_____
_____
_____
_____
_____
_____

Even sleepers are workers and collaborators on what goes on in the universe.

—HERACLITUS, *THE COSMIC FRAGMENTS*

Remembrances

_____

_____

_____

_____

_____

_____

_____

_____

_____

_____

_____

_____

_____

_____

_____

_____

_____

_____

_____

_____

_____

Reminders

Do Your work in me, Father, as I sleep...

I will praise the LORD, who counsels me; even at night my heart instructs me. I have set the LORD always before me. Because he is at my right hand, I will not be shaken. Therefore my heart is glad and my tongue rejoices; my body also will rest secure.

—PSALM 16:7-9

Remembrances

_____

_____

_____

_____

_____

_____

_____

_____

_____

_____

_____

_____

_____

_____

_____

_____

_____

_____

_____

_____

_____

_____

Some thoughts wear combat boots at night
and stomp around my brain. If You're not trying to gain my
attention, could You make them wear fuzzy house slippers?
Thank You. Amen.

"Turn your eyes upon Jesus, look full in His wonderful face…"

I wondered if she knew I was listening.

"and the cares of earth grow strangely dim…"

Her voice was sweet and gentle.

"in the light of His glory and grace."

—FROM "CLOISTERED," *STARDUST ON MY PILLOW*

Remembrances

_____
_____
_____
_____
_____
_____
_____
_____
_____
_____

Reminders

_____
_____
_____
_____
_____

Help me to turn my eyes upon You, Jesus...

_____
_____
_____
_____
_____
_____
_____

The net of the sleeper catches fish.

—GREEK PROVERB

Remembrances

_____

_____

_____

_____

_____

_____

_____

_____

_____

_____

_____

_____

_____

_____

_____

_____

_____

_____

_____

_____

_____

_____

_____

_____

_____
_____
_____
_____
_____
_____
_____
_____
_____
_____

Reminders

_____
_____
_____
_____
_____

Give me dreams that speak of You, Father,

_____
_____
_____
_____
_____
_____
_____
_____

It is hard to believe what a wide circle our lives make, reaching forward and back for generations. And yet we can be condensed down to ten boxes of belongings. How small we are and yet how lasting our influence.

—FROM "BOXED IN," *STARDUST ON MY PILLOW*

Remembrances

_____
_____
_____
_____
_____
_____
_____
_____
_____
_____

Reminders

_____
_____
_____
_____
_____

God, help me keep in mind how my life is worth so much and yet, at the same time, so little... _____
_____
_____
_____
_____
_____
_____

God made two great lights—the greater light to govern the day and the lesser light to govern the night. He also made the stars. God set them in the expanse of the sky to give light on the earth, to govern the day and the night, and to separate light from darkness. And God saw that it was good.

—GENESIS 1:16-18

Remembrances

_____

_____

_____

_____

_____

_____

_____

_____

_____

_____

_____

_____

_____

_____

_____

_____

_____

_____

_____

_____

_____

_____
_____
_____
_____
_____
_____
_____
_____
_____
_____

Reminders

_____
_____
_____
_____
_____

Good and gracious God, _____

_____
_____
_____
_____
_____
_____
_____
_____

Running away from your problems doesn't solve them.

—FROM "RUNAWAY," *STARDUST ON MY PILLOW*

Remembrances

_____

_____

_____

_____

_____

_____

_____

_____

_____

_____

_____

_____

_____

_____

_____

_____

_____

_____

_____

_____

_____

_____

_____

_____

_____

If I promise to apologize to you-know-who
tomorrow for my rude behavior, could I go to sleep now?
And, yes, I really am sorry. Amen.

And if tonight my soul may find her peace in sleep, and sink in
good oblivion, and in the morning wake like a new-opened
flower then I have been dipped again in God, and new created.

—D. H. LAWRENCE, *SHADOWS*

Remembrances

_____

_____

_____

_____

_____

_____

_____

_____

_____

_____

_____

_____

_____

_____

_____

_____

_____

_____

_____

_____

_____

_____

_____
_____
_____
_____
_____
_____
_____
_____
_____
_____

Make me a new-opened flower, Lord, _____

_____
_____
_____
_____
_____
_____
_____

A star will come out of Jacob; a scepter will rise out of Israel.

—Numbers 24:17

Remembrances

_____

_____

_____

_____

_____

_____

_____

_____

_____

_____

_____

_____

_____

_____

_____

_____

_____

_____

_____

_____

_____

_____

_____

_____

_____

_____

_____
_____
_____
_____
_____
_____
_____
_____
_____
_____

Reminders

_____
_____
_____
_____
_____

Dearest King of Israel, _____
_____
_____
_____
_____
_____
_____
_____

To sleep is to feast.

—PERSIAN PROVERB

Remembrances

_____

_____

_____

_____

_____

_____

_____

_____

_____

_____

Reminders

_____

_____

_____

_____

_____

Allow me to sink into the feast of rest, dear God,

_____

_____

_____

_____

_____

_____

_____

"You know, Lord, You could have rescued me! In a moment, You could have healed me. Where were You when I needed You?" Julya railed at the ceiling. Hearing her own feelings articulated both frightened and relieved her. She waited for the cabin to tumble down on her for such an outburst.

Instead, she heard within her a voice clearer than a mountain stream and purer than a baby's laughter. I was in the wise counsel of your doctors, the steady hands of your surgeon, the compassionate care of your nurses, the tears of your support group, and the love of your family. I sat through your office visits, I knelt at your bedside, I rejoiced in your recovery. I wept at your anger, and I felt your anguish.

—FROM "CHRISTMAS CABIN," *STARDUST ON MY PILLOW*

Remembrances

_____
_____
_____
_____
_____
_____
_____
_____
_____
_____
_____

Reminders

_____
_____
_____
_____
_____
_____

Constant Companion, _____

_____
_____
_____
_____
_____
_____
_____
_____
_____

People are too apt to treat God as if he were a minor royalty.

—SIR HERBERT BEERBOHM-TREE, QUOTED IN *BEERBOHM-TREE*

Remembrances

When Your Word comes to me suddenly

in the night, emblazoned on my mind, I am left breathless.

Imagine, You speaking to me. Amen.

You are all sons of God through faith in Christ Jesus, for all of you who were baptized into Christ have clothed yourselves with Christ. There is neither Jew nor Greek, slave nor free, male nor female, for you are all one in Christ Jesus. If you belong to Christ, then you are Abraham's seed, and heirs according to the promise.

—GALATIANS 3:26-29

Remembrances

_____

_____

_____

_____

_____

_____

_____

_____

_____

_____

Reminders

_____

_____

_____

_____

_____

_____

Thank You for the promise, Jesus, _____

_____

_____

_____

_____

_____

_____

_____

When I go to bed I leave my troubles in my clothes.

—DUTCH PROVERB

Remembrances

_____

_____

_____

_____

_____

_____

_____

_____

_____

_____

_____

_____

_____

_____

_____

_____

_____

_____

_____

_____

_____

_____

_____

_____

_____

_____

_____
_____
_____
_____
_____
_____
_____
_____
_____
_____

Reminders

_____
_____
_____
_____
_____

Lord, help me to lay my troubles aside and rest in You...

_____
_____
_____
_____
_____
_____
_____

Lord, I want my life to count, but most of my years are behind
me. Is there some way I could make up for all those lost years?
Or at least use the time I have left in significant ways? Lead me,
Lord, and help me to be wise enough to follow.

—FROM "THE WEDDING RING," *STARDUST ON MY PILLOW*

Remembrances

_____

_____

_____

_____

_____

_____

_____

_____

_____

_____

_____

_____

_____

_____

_____

_____

_____

_____

_____

_____

_____

_____

_____

_____

_____

_____

_____

_____

_____

_____

_____

_____

_____

_____

_____

Reminders

_____

_____

_____

_____

_____

Father of Time, You promise to give us back the years the moths and locusts destroy; help me to focus on my future… _____

_____

_____

_____

_____

_____

_____

If you want inner peace find it in solitude, not speed.

—STEWART L. UDALL, *THE QUIET CRISIS*

Remembrances

_____

_____

_____

_____

_____

_____

_____

_____

_____

_____

_____

_____

_____

_____

_____

_____

_____

_____

_____

_____

_____

_____

_____

_____

_____

_____

_____

_____

_____

_____

_____

_____

_____

_____

_____

Reminders

_____

_____

_____

_____

_____

Show me the way, God, to find time to draw away and be with You... _____

_____

_____

_____

_____

_____

_____

I wonder if wisdom

pays visits in the night

because sometimes it's the only time

we're still enough to hear?

Collecting Stardust

Some of my most splendid thoughts started as a spark in the night; it might have been whispers from heaven, ideas for a book, resolution for a lingering problem, insight for a friend, a poem, a prayer worth repeating, etc. I used to believe when nighttime thoughts came to me, "This is so profound I'll never forget it," and then I'd drift off to sleep. The next morning would arrive with the annoying realization that those incredible insights—the ones that would never leave me—had vanished, leaving a nagging frustration in their place. Try as I might, I couldn't force the thoughts back into my conscious mind. At best I pulled up fragments, which is why I found Collecting Stardust to be so helpful.

Recently I awoke in the wee hours with a poem moving around in my heart. I knew if I slept on it I might lose the creative inspiration of the moment. So I rose up, grabbed a pen and my journal, and dashed off the lines. I'm so pleased I did, because the Lord has used it in some unexpected and sweet ways.

I remember once when the following thought entered my mind, "A wise woman waits." At the time, I couldn't imagine to what it pertained, but ever since it has been an ongoing word of counsel for me in a myriad of situations. I'm grateful I collected that dazzling stardust by writing it down.

I wonder if wisdom pays visits in the night because sometimes it's the only time we're still enough to hear? Hmm, something to contemplate… Whatever the reason(s), let's not allow the speckles of stardust that are sprinkled into our minds to lose their brilliance but instead be wise enough to collect them.

COLLECTING

Date: _____
Stardust Inspiration: _____
_____
_____
_____

Date: _____
Stardust Inspiration: _____
_____
_____
_____

Date: _____
Stardust Inspiration: _____
_____
_____
_____

Date: _____
Stardust Inspiration: _____
_____
_____
_____
_____

Date: _____
Stardust Inspiration: _____
_____
_____
_____

STARDUST

Date: _____

Stardust Inspiration: _____
_____
_____
_____

Date: _____

Stardust Inspiration: _____
_____
_____
_____

Date: _____

Stardust Inspiration: _____
_____
_____
_____

Date: _____

Stardust Inspiration: _____
_____
_____
_____

Date: _____

Stardust Inspiration: _____
_____
_____
_____

COLLECTING

Date: _____

Stardust Inspiration: _____

_____

_____

_____

Date: _____

Stardust Inspiration: _____

_____

_____

_____

Date: _____

Stardust Inspiration: _____

_____

_____

_____

Date: _____

Stardust Inspiration: _____

_____

_____

_____

Date: _____

Stardust Inspiration: _____

_____

_____

_____

STARDUST

Date: _____
Stardust Inspiration: _____
_____
_____
_____

Date: _____
Stardust Inspiration: _____
_____
_____
_____

Date: _____
Stardust Inspiration: _____
_____
_____
_____

Date: _____
Stardust Inspiration: _____
_____
_____
_____

Date: _____
Stardust Inspiration: _____
_____
_____
_____

COLLECTING

Date: _____
Stardust Inspiration: _____
_____
_____
_____

Date: _____
Stardust Inspiration: _____
_____
_____
_____

Date: _____
Stardust Inspiration: _____
_____
_____
_____

Date: _____
Stardust Inspiration: _____
_____
_____
_____

Date: _____
Stardust Inspiration: _____
_____
_____
_____

STARDUST

Date: _____
Stardust Inspiration: _____
_____
_____
_____

Date: _____
Stardust Inspiration: _____
_____
_____
_____

Date: _____
Stardust Inspiration: _____
_____
_____
_____

Date: _____
Stardust Inspiration: _____
_____
_____
_____

Date: _____
Stardust Inspiration: _____
_____
_____
_____

BUSINESS PLANS ARE FORMED ★ HOPES ARE BIRTHED ★ DREAMS